LOST POEMS

Marc Savett

NFB
Buffalo, New York

ISBN: 978-0-9978317-5-7

Lost Poems/Savett-1st ed.
1. Poems. 2. Poetry. 3. Verse.
4. Savett

Cover photograph courtesy of the author

No Frills Buffalo/Amelia Press
<<<>>>
119 Dorchester Road
Buffalo, New York 14213
For more information please visit
nfbpublishing.com

To Spike who walked his time a poet

LOST POEMS

Contents

LAREDO TO OKLAHOMA CITY

Low beams cut through the fog
Flowing over three inches of
Hail cooling the high mountain
Road, the silver MG's engine
Was gasping for
Air, flying at 65mph, roof
down,
Arrhythmias playing with our hearts.

She said bad karma was flowing through the gas
Pedal beneath cloudless patches,
Where hydrogen was burning to
Starlight, cylinders begged for gas,
Fighting the resistance of cold mountain air
Pushing the black horn,
A circular convexity on the
Dashboard, flushed out shadows.

She was breathing
Hard, hot with liquid
Passion,
Sinking deep into the leather seat,
Lusty with soft fingers
The windshield breaking the
Wind; faces frozen,
Stars like sequins—
Sparkling through apertures of open sky.

SATCHELS OF DOUBT

Imagining his flesh on fire—
Held tight, like a butterfly—
Pinned to the salty earth,
Diving tasks deep in earnest
Devotion to strings and bow
Transcending prisons bored routine,
Years evaporate into fog and flood.

Friends disappear to ashy air,
Carrying the planet on solar
Wind in satchels holding doubt
On shoulders that can bear forced weight.
Looking back toward broken
Promises of a small town,
Past fields whistling messages in the winds.

Ringing in the ears, suggesting
Memories, soft faces marching through
His eyes; daydreams of a young
Argonaut playing with the protractor
Changing dimensions of the brain
Stretching through distant outposts.

FASCIST'S REVENGE

Fascists had rummaged through my valise,
Cashing away magazines.
When I opened the backpack it looked like a
Maniac had pillaged my very soul.
I boarded a bus in Lisbon; the rag-women put
Their evil eyes all over me,
Tying me in knots,
Berating my long hair in Portuguese.

The night before I walked the beach drunk with red wine;
In a Lisbon bar later I stared into embers in the fireplace.
Transience de jour as they were sucked up the flue with images of
the Fascists.

Staring at my magazines with sex-starved eyes
As fear was nibbling at my heels,
Wondering when they would break down my door,
Then take me into custody.

Now they all knew my secrets as I bolted down the stairway
To the lobby and street; I stood naked in Madrid,
Imagining a dank Spanish Inquisition.
As I walked for a hour losing track of the
hotel's
Address—my ladies were gone.

I took a cab to the Prado Museum, resting before
Velazquez' The Maids Of Honor, with its freaky women
Bringing me back to the raison d'etre
Of my own journey; running from the claustrophobia of
My family that shook me, like standing in front of
A firing squad in an el Greco
As fascists followed me as fireworks fell from the black night sky.

LATIN TEACHER

Miss Peters, a Latin Teacher, famous for her
Eccentricity, wore tight sweaters,
Which accentuated large breasts.

One afternoon, she began fiddling
With a garnet earring on her left earlobe.
She was oblivious
To the snickering of her classroom.
Briefly she fumbled with the earring,
Before losing it between her breasts.

As if no one else were present,
She pushed her hand
Between her breasts,
Sweeping and groping for the jewel.

The situation then evolved
Badly: a falsie dislodged
From her right breast.
There was the earring and
Falsie, like the earth and moon
Revolving around each other,
With her hand a satellite
Wobbling out of control
At the level of her belly.

Suddenly she sighed
As she grabbed the earring;
She eased the falsie
Back to its rightful place,
Then pulled her hand from
The depths of despair,

Straightening herself with one

Final pull of her sweater,
She smiled at her class
And then began reading her
Latin book,
Preparing for the next lesson.

THE NAKED LADY

Fate is the little lady that plants a kiss
On the lips of a man careening toward the cliff.

I meet him as he is being shackled to a metal table
By a guard, silent, dressed in black,
As if this is a funeral and not an interview.

Eight rectangular windows in the hall
Of the prison reflect the weight room,
With large benches holding Olympic bar bells
With posters of men with massive muscle
Growth on their pecs, biceps and deltoids.

The imprisoned is a goldfish with great bulging eyes
Coming to the surface to breathe
Oxygen from the heavy air,
As the guards rush into long
Halls from their sequestered spaces.
They inspect my identification clipped to my lapel.

The prisoner is tense, knowing I'm interviewing
Him to determine whether he can stand trial;
He describes the problems in his life
That resulted in his arrest.

The sad man across the table sees himself as
A family man, as he shares secrets of battery and rape—
Difficult to reconcile with his representation.

He paints for me a primitive remorse as he clowns;
Earlier he met with a public defender
Who has sixteen offenders swimming in his
Brain—the accused can't remember his lines
Or appreciate his terrible acting

That freaks the breath from his audience

He is a foul smelling man, with a canal like
Scar on the left side of his head
That occurred in a bar scuffle,
A beer bottle opening his skull.

The reverberations in the small
Room strain hearing.
The naked lady sits on his palm,
Magnifying his weakness with her weight.

I look through his broken home,
Distant family, and genetic limitations
As he sits across from me in his orange wrinkled prison garb,
Attached with chain link to a table
As I review his life.

I watch other prisoners speaking to loved ones by phone,
Incarcerated behind thick glass panes,
Listening to their families' regrets and aspirations
Heartened by the sweet familiar voices
That open dark constricted passageways.

SHACKLES OF THE MIND

He sinks into a funk torn by a misdemeanor
Decades past; sharing the story carelessly with colleagues
Could ruin a reputation.

The small tick that hangs on your
Lifeblood never falls from the carrier—
An error of youth becomes an irresistible force.
Over time a boy, now a man, is flashed back
To the flashing red lights in the driveway;
There is a harsh knocking at the door,
Officers comb the house for contraband
Like the Red Guard.

Fifty years later the event is written on the
Perimeter of a barred iron cell.
There remains a virtual tattoo inked on the
Chest; any effort to expunge the charges
Draws one deeper into exposure and risk.

The shadow of the law is a long darkness;
One who attempts to exonerate himself
Falls deeper into a silent pit.

An indiscretion of youth continues to
Shackle the potential of an old man.

ANEMONES OF SPRINGTIME

The marriage was a trembler:
She was the Liz Taylor,
Her husband a Richard Burton.

They were both models of the 1950's when gas
was cheap,
The war was over,
And euphoria flowed over the land.
There were fifty years
Of births, deaths, insecurities and
drama.

She could exhibit her specimens to close
acquaintances,
Who she could please with her glowing intellect
That sparkled from the furrows in her forehead;
There was always art that grew up through her genetic
material,
Painting the landscape into a diffuse pointillism.

Yellow canaries sang themselves free
Of their cages—
Friends were drawn to her eccentricities,
Concentric circles shimmering with gossamers of
poetry.
She blossomed like anemones in the spring-time; deaths
receded.

They were easy to forget in June,
When she strolled among the pitcher plants,
Poppies, and spinning maple seeds.
Her pleasure was colorful blooms
Bursting about her like revolving planets;
She read the palm of the mighty firmament
For clues for her own salvation.

LES PAUL GUITAR

Marty is a placid individual,
Impervious to the outside world.
Not quite important enough
To bring him to a boil—
However, there are objects dear,
Specifically his Les Paul guitars.
Would he part with his ultimate axe?

As my mouth watered, thinking of the
Melodies flying off the Les Paul,
I fantasized the guitar with maple top
Rosewood finger board
And steely humbucker pick-ups.

He explained politely that
One of his guitars has a certain honk;
Another a growl;
A third a wicked quack;
Another a sound sweet like honey;
The fifth a violin sustain that lasted for days;
The last a beauty like a black swan that if it
were sold,
Would result in his wife bringing
All the terrors in the world upon him.

It was clear that separating him
From his guitars would be like tearing his heart
Out, all the vital parts sewn into the mandala
Of his spirit.

WALK TO THE MALL

My parents sent my brothers off to the strip mall.
They were drawn to the pet shop that specialized
In fresh water tropical fish,
Carrying also a stack of current rock albums;
Jake was directed to accompany Isaac
Down the hill to the shopping center,
And return walking up the hill until both were safely home.

Jake soon lost interest in the role of monitor,
Venturing from his appointed task.
Isaac was nearly home after the long climb
When an older man asked him if he needed a ride.

Isaac was eight years—evil but an abstract
concept—
Mr. Pink laughed, telling the boy he was his cousin
As he drove past the house to the town park.
My brother found himself in the province of Sodom,
where he was abused.

Isaac confided many years later that
His death seemed imminent.
Maybe it was Jake's guilt
Of abandonment of his charge
That led to incursions with pot and alcohol.

Perhaps it was Isaac's
Error in judgement, Jumping
pell-mell into
The chariot with the Devil
When mother coached both
brothers
To walk straight home,
That broke his confidence.

Lugging the burden of humiliation,
A lifetime.

DEEP WOUNDS

Deep wounds infect the inner city like
A twenty five year flu; kids in their prime
Michael,
Freddie,
And Tamir,
Live in a world of broken doors, shattered aspirations,
Talkin' the talk, dark faces in a world of gun fighters.

Throwing off chains, flames owning the street—
The smartest walk through the ghetto with half
answers,
Throwing money bags of nothing, slums as ruins,
Vigilantes breathe smoke and fire igniting gasoline.

The breath of the volcano, running guns and heroin;
Cities lost in curfew after curfew, fighting battles that
Tear at America's heart, warring with itself, refighting
Vietnam
And the Civil War like a never ending nightmare.

Earthquakes of hatred; two hundred years of
Blood sport—America lost in a spiral of forgetting
As cops own the poor, beating down the masses
Angry, obscene, broken into sand
Until they become Molotov cocktails of resistance.

Ears deaf—eyes blind—speech jumbled—fireworks incite,
Seditious tidal waves falling on the metropolis;
Great cities succulent devoured from the middle.

ROCK AND ROLLERS

There was madness in the roadhouse—
Women dancing with women, Following hormones,
Picking the guy fingering a guitar
Who was paying explicit Attention to the sweet peaches.

Gyrating in tight jeans—
With loose blouses without morals—
Traveling down a highway,
An orgy pinned like butterflies
To the backseat moaning soft pleasures.

Liberating under-age behavior—
Nakedness, blind to the music,
Stirring dancers to strut,
Then scream their impotence
To escape the wildness.

Infected by the beam of rock and roll,
Clinging tight to naked waists
Begging anatomy lessons locked
Eye to eye into the tension
Of the substance of their future.

PHOTOGRAPHIC MEMORY

Walking through Times Square,
Flashing big screen breaking news;
Thoughts percolating like black coffee,
Waking the brain.

Taxis, cats with four claws, flying to a
stop;
Shops full of estate jewelry—
Diamonds, emeralds, and dragon flies—
Musicians and poets kick peanut shells
On the coffee house floor.

Alan Ginsberg recites a mantra
While playing a table.
Classmates turn on a wheel,
Holding photos of twelve years
With many empty spaces
Dissolving into background;
You shadowbox like Carmen Basilio,
Champion of the world,
Punching at the air.

I'm lost in a collection of thirty
Blue Morpho butterflies
That will never fly to distant forests.
Market quotes rock and roll
On a ticker as hyenas comb the landscape
For their share.

Waifs run the dirty streets for guns and candy;
Roosters crow as dogs howl in the morning;
An anchor sits on my chest.

Death's face marches to drums in the distance—
A prince places a gold ring
On the duchess' finger.

He walks with a limp,
Reflexes losing their position
In the universe,
A young woman looks into his
Eyes as if she knows him.

PORNOGRAPHIC WORD

War is the most dangerous word.
A cobra slithering over civility,
Countries devour themselves
Like beasts contesting the antelope;
There are inescapable massacres,
Insurrections and terror.

The heart turns petrified,
Deprived of bread and water,
Bringing starvation and wailing.

A million people killed in Leningrad:
"Forty-three thousand libraries,
Eighty-four thousand schools,
And forty-thousand hospitals"*
Crumpled to dust in World War II;
War circles the earth in Misery.

At eight-fifteen on a placid morning
In Hiroshima, Japan,
LITTLE BOY exploded, killing over
One hundred thousand people—
Swallowed by the graveyard.

Diamonds and guns are currency
As the great migrations follow the sun;
Strong absorb the weak,
Tactical advantage is a slippery roulette wheel.

The wildebeest finds no peace
Facing the lion, then the crocodiles
At the crossroads of the Mara River.

We are Lost in Iraq;
Lost in Afghanistan;
Lost in Vietnam;
Lost in Syria;
Lost in Pakistan;
Lost in Israel;
Lost in America;
Lost in ourselves.

The military industrial complex
Supports the brick-bodied fighters
Who tote the weapons bravely,
Battling through casualty and cruelty,
Prisoners to hellish experience;
Marching through South-East Asia,
Marching through Gettysburg,
Marching through Normandy,
Marching through Iwo Jima—
Hearing the voices and whispers
Telling the tales as they
Walk among the frozen faces.

HOT HOT DAYS

There are the hot, hot days;
Life is expanded,
Orchids loose with fragrant grace,
Swans dive through the online banks.

They quench thirst for immediate gratification.
Jeans, diamonds, and glitter shoes
March through the door;
Then comes the exit
Of the orphaned to sales shelves,
A blink—then snow patterns,
The roof in mosaics.

Winter storms constricting
Crowds to splinters of ice,
Dead batteries and sputtering spark plugs
Numb the gas pedal.

Heat cranked from the furnace
Finds opening through blankets
Wrapped like mummies
Before the big screen,
While darkness sits heavy on the chest
Under naked boughs
As crows call a winter song
Longing for the hot, hot days.

GOLDEN MELODIES

The painted horse cantered into the
Golden sunset that took our breath.
Hoofs slipped over the perilous boulder face,
Finding their balance;
The horses shook their large heads,
Trumpeting their presence,
Echoing through the canyon.

A split second reverie,
Sharing a glass of wine
With a dark eyed black haired beauty,
Might end with a stallion disappearing
Into thin air down a canyon wall.

Once in the valley,
You can squeeze your legs tight to the belly,
Hugging the neck as a lover,
Galloping into yellow light;
Recalling failure now, tomorrow's
success.

Melodies of Bach's English Suite float through ears.
You look back at the horses tied to their posts,
Stuck in commitments at the wooden hut.
A leathery handed cook gives you a liver burrito
With refried beans that never tasted so good
On a parched throat dosed mightily
With a cool bottle of Dos Equis.

JACK-KNIFE

The ship bursts with humanity;
It travels like the hands of a clock
Circumventing the oceans.
Becoming cognizant, it is apparent
That people fall in the vessel's wake.

We begin to appreciate the gravity of loss;
There are gaps of absence
Imprinted on memory—
They disappear in a line to a point
On the horizon, drawn in silence.
We feel the emptiness of their space,
Since the dead reflect the
Accomplishments of the living.

We focus on the colors
Of sun and moon,
Shimmering on the surface of life.

You do not forget how love
Whispered in your ear
As the ship separates the waves;
One hears their faint splash
As we focus on the reflections
Of those known
Who have branded us deep.
Another jack-knifes from the deck,
Falling through the breakers.

CIRCLES OF CRYSTAL

The white birch had patches of snow
That coated her boughs.

Standing over the pond,
Snow fell as ice crystalized
To a slippery brick.

The boy shoveled as his father watched;
Soon a small rink was done.
The skates' blades painted pictures
In concentric circles of crystal—
The child's face glowed,
His stick feigning to and fro
Toward an illusory net
As he inhaled the cold air.

The rink grew as the snow was pushed
Away to the calls of black crows
On a branch laughing.

The boy's smile was lost in daydream,
Imagining he was the most famous hockey player
That ever lived
As his team skated round him
Staring in frozen admiration
As a light snow fell on the ice.

THROUGH NITE

You touch me deep,
Without fanfare
Or brass bands marching.

Soft shivers from fingers
That tickle the funny bone,
That bone recalcitrant;
Unruly eyes lost in deep eyes,
Laugh on laugh,
Feeling lightness
Of smile within smile.

Flickering glance, connected to the
Candle of the universe;
The night pouring sparkling
Light revelations chardonnay,
Hands through hands
With lips on lips,
Leaving no evidence
But a taste of memory.

Pouring a hundred butterflies
Into the dark night—
The airliner quiet,
Purring like a cat
Descending into Paris.

NAUTILUS SONG

If you decide to listen to the
Message of the conch shell
For a lifetime of meditation,
Then probably you will find more solace
Listening to the contents of a mailbox.

The shell blooms in pearly opalescence
Though crumbles into small chips
Without the nourishment of the sea;
Each generation adds its luster to the organic whole,
Layer upon layer.

Inside the beauty, edginess is pervasive;
Shadows lengthen while
Sea worms search for shelter.

Hackers break down barriers
While false prophets seek
Messiahs immune from contagion.

She calls my name as they decode signs;
Threats abound through the porous borders,
As they dissect the chambered nautilus
For answers to their profound questions.

CHOCOLATE MOUSSE AT NOON

She said there was a tear in the fabric of existence.
Black tights and nylon to protect the legs from rude stares
Was the reply.

Dear, I am so looking forward to chocolate mousse,
With the blackest chocolate at noon.

There must be a fire or a shooting,
With the music of sirens signing their tenor—
Waking up sky scrapers
Poking through the wrinkled clouds.

Darling the news is so dour:
Nothing but obscure individuals
Trying to find themselves,
Behaving in the most venal manner.

All etiquette was lost after 9/11
In a glue of sadness;
The singers are so self-absorbed.
The nuanced humor in a song now escapes me;
There are only bad boys playing games
That draw delinquent pre-pubescent females.

It's so easy to lose yourself behind a Halloween mask,
Behaving like a ghoul—
Though much harder to hide bad deeds
Behind every day faces.
Where have all the flowers gone, Pete Seeger?

WAR'S PROMISE

Occupiers sit in the master bedroom;
The countess begs for divorce,
Combing her long black hair before the mirror.

She is a butterfly gifting hope
To the dispossessed—
Couriers allow her to sit on their shoulders.
Everything below seems locked in convulsion;
Sadness flows down the mountains,
War growls like a tarantula,
Feasting on the face of the world.

Families split apart into elemental atoms,
Speech is amplified into disoriented terror.
The smoke of suffering wafts through windows;
Ambassadors give freedom for her diamonds.

Tears flow down her cheeks
As she shimmers in moonlight,
War keeps no promises
As she punches her ticket to freedom.

GOLDEN CAVE

You are not alone.
I am by your side.

You call me an infidel,
Though I am an explorer of emptiness;
My tears rain over the Italian landscape,
Vision blurred from the castle's parapet.
I am the sun; you the earth,
Dragons passing in the night,
Eclipsing the moon.

Melodies play through piccolo beaks
That snap the seed;
Nuthatches, white-gray, crawl audible
Brittle boughs.
They flicker into the stark
Naked winter twilight.

You appear out of a shimmering veil;
The golden cave is covered in thick moss,
In fragrant fields of trillium.

We lose ourselves in reinvention,
Drugged in opium excursion,
As we lie in bed tangled in flannel sheets
And Amish quilt.

Your dark hair falls over a down pillow
As you sleep-talk of shadows on walls,
Spelling tales as they dance on moonlight.
Just as the alarm wakes a Vivaldi Concerto,
As earth spins to the day.

GRACE FROM THE WOLVES

The sun carries the planets through the
Milky Way because she must;
Boundaries change through war,
Then armistice brings the forgetting
Oceans rise and fall
To the tune of sine wave,
Strings played by the moon.

If the mistakes are repeated
It must be the mistake's fault;
Sisyphus carries the rock up, Then down the
craggy peaks.

The calculus is clear
That you will cross an electric fence in
Life, the boundary that faces
Forward and backwards.

Living inside those burdens we bear
As the heart is lost to the stone's weight,
Ingenuity gives up a spark
That may offer the shepherd
Another day's grace from the wolves.

If you are the color, you must stay within the lines
Or run into choppy weather;
One climbs as high as he might,
Though there will only be air to grab.
If you are living beyond oxygen,
You will fall from orbit,
Mesmerized by earth's beauty.

CRIMES OF PASSION

What she was is not who she is:
Accused of aberrations,
Dishonored by incrimination,
Catching glimpses of historical scenes
That mortify with remembrance
Photos pinned to memory's wall.

Shame that others may know,
The push-pull of pubescent politics,
Self-conscious hiding behind biology experiments;
Kissing in the bush, she spits out monsters
That inhabit the dark zone,
Engorged with promises played forever
Until a rascal exposes secret love,
Crimes of passion.

Birds and bees pollinate the delphinium;
Mirrors reflect through the mind
What a woman was, is now
An illusion of who she's become.

Sloughing skins wearing different uniforms:
Lovers' reflections mirroring to infinity.

EXORCISM OF THE MUFFLER IMPS

The catalytic convertor is a magic furnace.
That pulls the putrid smells of damnation
Through her lips,
Like a deep drag on a cigarette,
Saturating the lungs with blackness
While turning the thickened exhaust to a clear essence.

The shaking and knocking of the devil dogs
Howling and scratching is stripped
Of its crushing effect on the breath;
Vampires and bats fly back to their dark caverns,
Banging and jerking gradually relents.

The cabin is freed from choking combustions;
Lungs clear like fog breaking across the valley.
Headlights shine like two moonbeams
Upon the highway slipping behind.

BURNT WITH POISON

Incidents stand like sign posts
As one crawls through the brambles,
Trying to get an arm around life.

A friend's father drove off bandits
Below the border on the road to Jalisco
With a Colt 45;
Fear was paralyzing,
With death's threatening breath.

Cows owned the road at midnight
As two brothers were killed
On the road to Loredo,
Crashing into the bottom of a canyon.

There were many people I ran with
Through harrowing experiences
As pieces of the puzzle pulled a shape
For the future
That became a predictable constellation
In the night sky.

I've seen people burnt with poison—
Some died from abandonment and shame;
Anyone of a thousand I've met
Could have been the one,
With the dice gone cold.

PRANKS FROM THE EDGE OF NOTHINGNESS

We run with the clowns that hinge to our funny bone;
Their painted faces and oversize shoes
Push, cackle, and provoke sensibility.
Creamy faces barter for snuff or a smoke.
They mug for an audience floating by with sad eyes.

Crowds are paralyzed by the sustained barrage of one-liners
That brings the strongest to tears.
These funny men cachet themselves away,
Reinventing new personas—
They are masters of deflecting bullets of criticism
Back at the sender.

We barely notice them until we find ourselves
Bursting in the belly with their jabs and jokes;
They look into the void with clown eyes,
The earth spinning as they grab a prank
From the edge of nothingness.

SPRINGS IN THE DESERT

Great Grandfather left his wife one day
Without a trace.
My mother's father was a tough, one-sided man
Who worked hard in his Army & Navy store;
His wife made him dinner;
He then sat in front of the black and white TV,
Watching a western or two
While sipping Scotch Whiskey.

My grandfather came to America
From Eastern Europe,
Never learning English,
But speaking better Yiddish.

He often sat apart from others—
Humming folkloric melodies—
Finding security in his private place.

His son and daughter-in-law
Engaged in corporeal punishment
And magical thinking,
Certain their son would be
Accepted to Harvard.
He made elegant silver and gold bridges
That filled empty spaces between teeth.

The women in my life speak in code;
Often times I turn off to it
Because it becomes loud and strident,
Hurting my ears.

All of these people
Could have dug deeper in the sand,
For there are springs that run
Under the desert.

WAREHOUSE WEDDING

Windows steel the light,
Reflecting it like a mirror
Caught by gravity,
Shot full of bosons—
Giving weight to floating thought
That dives off the lips.

Meeting eye to eye,
Names marching past
One by one,
Wearing tuxedos
On the red carpet.

Waiting for the ceremony:
Will you take this man?
Will you take this woman?
Into an electromagnetic trust,
With a safety deposit box—
That holds three keys—
That opens portals
To the family catacombs.

They stand with strict coiffure,
Holding vodka and orange juice in toast,
As the best man steps forward
With shaky hands.
Jesters that give laughter and lightness,
As Pablo Neruda's poetry
Recedes backward into the universe.

EXODUS

Julia begged for salvation;
Just a hack to the chains around an ankle,
Her Siamese cat nestled into her lap.

Cooing chirping sounds rose
Like a flute concerto;
Blue eyes flashed about the room,
The hook cinched through her lower lip,
A librarian bouncing between
Exhaustion and loneliness.

Through strings of tomorrows
There were consequences
When uncapping volcanoes—
Abandoning the island could be
Just a chain of lonesome islands,
The daily grind oppressed.

Though she was fearful of lighting
The fuse of anarchy,
When she read poetry suffocation relented.
Like a whale, she tweeted love songs across oceans,
Unable to abandon her lair.

She lost herself in black and white movies
As the Siamese purred softly,
Staring deep into her eyes.

MARINARA

Though the moon is crazy—
Shining its drusy, milky light
On lovers kissing—
Earth spins around its axis,
Never satiated
With her diet of evil,
Served with Barbaresco daily.

In the guise of assassinations,
Starvation, coups, and invasions,
Filling the earth's palate
With tasty pan broil
In marinara—a feast
She just can't seem
To get enough of.

CHAINED TO TRUTHS

He was accused of transgressions:
Breaking the tablets,
Unholy violations.
Three strikes, and chains forever.

His valves of memory
Spray torrents of steam, Regrets of his move
folding
His poker hand,
Beaten by fate's straight flushes.

Never serving hard time:
Just eternal probation,
Tied like a noose around the neck,
A nightmare chained by spikes To a granite cliff,
Attracting a vulture that
Picks at the bones daily.

Foul deeds exaggerated by harsh time
That will not speak clearly,
Leaving him a fish flopping on the shore,
Abandoned by the sea.

He laughs at a thousand incidents,
A loop of luck
That lifted him over beds of nails,
Crucifixions and iron bars;
Near misses by cosmic debris
That could have turned reality farther south,
Scattering birds through withered hours.
But then, he's walking briskly

Down the halls of his day—
Respected in employment,

Defying a few bad breaks
Placed on time served.
Chained forever to past truths
That bend the back,
Then break the heart.

EARTH ATTRACTION

I am slowing down— Or maybe the earth is.
I notice she stares at times;
I become self-conscious,
And look away.

There's always been this infatuation
We've had for one another.
But why would she reciprocate now,
In my waning years,
When I haven't the energy—
To plow her fields,
Excavate deep wells,
Mine precious minerals,
Taste exotic liquids—
That could give us both pleasure?

She certainly is a seductress
Hard to ignore;
She warms me in my dreams,
As I explode into her day,
Losing myself in her deep blue eyes
Like oceans gently nudging
Against her lovely sleeping valleys.

KAFKA EXPERT

I know I have a wife
Like I have a right hand;
Her name, I think, is Doris—
Which has a pleasing rhyme.

I can describe my house:
It has cherry cabinets
In the dining room.

I know I am confusion.
There is a strange, distant sensation
Of my skull having a pulsing hole, In a space where brain
tissue
Used to reside.

I enjoy riding the lawn mower.
I can give you a tour of the upstairs:
There is a large bath
With a spa,
Where my wife is preening herself—
Like a bird
Combing spring feathers.

Guests will soon arrive
For the book club;
I can smell the thick scent
Of brie and mushrooms.

Arlene and Jason,
Our children,
Are at a basketball game.
I am an English professor—
A Kafka expert—

Floating on an iceberg,
Farther out to sea.
Looking back at brain surgery,
I am just a beetle
Hanging from the ceiling,
Blood rushing away From my body;
I have grown cold
Walking barefoot through clouds.

We have no mower,
Or children.
There is no book club Or spa—
Only illusions.

Days lose themselves,
As tears falling down my cheeks;
There is still a drive,
A spark of fire to create.

I pen dramas
That I forget as dreams.
This is a theatre of the damned;
I'm easily discouraged,
As scenarios of story
Fall to a purgatory of absurdity.
Permanence is merely
The flickering of unclear form.

I believe all I have in the end
Is Doris, children, and home,
But tragically I don't see anything
With clarity.

I'm not recalling much;

Maybe I have only
Something else...

Perhaps it's nothing—
No Doris, children or home.
It's a pervasive wave
Of loneliness,
As if I'm the last person
In the world.

I am an English professor.

INFATUATION

For two weeks, I was infatuated with a
Beautiful woman;
I wanted her in every way.
To run my fingers through her jet black hair,
And touch her breasts.

She could only talk of the vitality
Of her boyfriend
As we lay in the grass, holding each other;
She pushed me away with gentle shoves,
Bragging about his endless prowess—
Intercourse of magical proportions,
An even dozen times a day.

I knew then I was lying
Next to a goddess
That I could never touch
Without bringing
Grave consequences
From the gods to me,
A mere mortal.

RODENTS AND LICE

He was a dangerous dreamer of magic words
That fell through his fingers, diamonds and sand.
He envisioned penny novels that would write themselves,
Which were never more than sputtering animations
Across his windows that quickly fell to the night.

The kid seemed lost, though canaries sang
As they flittered about braiding his hair.
He felt gobbled by chimera, loping along
Lonely high peaks.

A hunter shooting arrows
To bag magic beasts that might change his luck,
Chasing fixes in angry neighborhoods,
Running from grotesque predatory creatures;
He slept more, turning stones to pilfer dreams
That might give him seven good years,
Waking too many nights to television fuzz.

His relativity was skewed
With visions of closing in on the planet of novels,
Though he was further than ever
From sitting down with his pen and typewriter.

He woke from a nightmare
Where he was smoking a joint in a meth lab,
As a professor handed him a degree in terror;
He lived on iced tea and sugar cubes
Laced with magic potions,
While his dreams became infested with rodents and lice
That devoured his novels nascent and pure.

IN IRONS ON A SUMMER EVENING

My wife made arrangements with friends
For a sail on Chautauqua Lake;
It was a lovely, warm, late summer evening.

I swam to the mooring, unfastening the shackle;
Our guests were walking past the clubhouse,
Carrying a bottle of Pinot Noir.
The boat was tied to the end of the dock.

We were sitting in the cockpit
As I cast off into a slight breeze;
The boat, as if possessed by an unkind spirit,
Floated lazily between two docks, forty yards apart.
We were caught in irons as if we were a car that revs,
But never shifted gear.

We drank the wine, making several trips between the docks.
The sailboat was like a whirly bug—
A compass tracing the same pattern for forty-five minutes.

Our friends had enough;
They disembarked the boat,
As if they had another engagement
after the sail.

At that moment, a former commodore
Was walking up the dock;
I implored him to help us escape this wicked spirit
That had pirated the boat.

He adjusted his cap, advising me to simply
Lower the center board,
Just as Gary Johnson, on page 18 in
How to Sail Had advised,

"With your sails up, your rudder in position,
Put your center board all the way down."

I swallowed hard, after spending an evening in irons
In three feet of water,
Quite close to shore.
My wife and I walked silently to the car

HALLOWEEN

It was Halloween time, the end of
October Corn stalks in the windows;
Kids would soon be soaping windows,
Stringing rolls of toilet paper in trees,
And pushing cars on lawns.

Our parents were dining at a friend's home.
It was Friday night—
The local television vampire "The Baron"
Was filling All Hallows Eve with a medley
Of horror films.

We were hearing crackling, groans, and moans
Coming from the large bar-room
In the basement.

We grabbed kitchen knives to protect ourselves;
Off the bar-room there was a small backroom,
Filled with bowling pins and large wooden boxes
That suggested crypts
That smelled dank with death.

Soon, my parents were knocking at the door;
They were clearly puzzled by the knives
In our hands.

We responded in unison
That we heard creepy noises in the basement—
We were quite sure that we heard conversation
Coming from the small backroom.

How could we ever protect ourselves without weapons
From Dracula, Frankenstein and the Werewolf, who were
Most certainly plotting behind the door in the backroom
Our demise?

SOUTHERN EXPOSURE

There's an oil painting that intrigues me at the museum.
The artist, Ryan, was killed in a tragic scuba-diving
accident.
He has rendered paradise as Picasso might:
A male nude is seated reading in a beach chair,
The female is reclining below him to the right,
naked—
Erotic with her protuberant breasts and buttocks.

It is a southern island with a yellow-white
sun
Beaming down on a sailboat on blue water,
Under intense blue sky.

They appear a serene couple, but they are
frozen
Like a computer page,
As if their brains are infected with spyware and Trojan
horses;
It is a paradise in paradox.

They plead for a security scan,
As if they've just placed a 'for sale' sign on their two-story
condo.
There are cracks in the painting
That have become more prominent in the past
year;
Ryan has surely haunted this work.

The next time I visit the museum I envision the couple
No longer in the frame, their property foreclosed,
The canvas a blank screen.

PARADISE

It's events most dear
That can cause considerable damage,
Like gluttony that gradually
Consumes the body
If there is no restraint.

The sons of the military family
May wear their honor to their grave;
You buy the sporty BMW
Only to be trapped in the front seat
By recklessness.

Counter-phobic tendencies
Drive you to climb steep mountain-faces
That may no longer accept your grip;
The trainer loves his tigers,
Who only see him as a possible meal.

One loves to fly—though cannot weather the storm
Crashing through the black night—
Where he meets the devil
Who promises a trip to paradise.

PRISONER

He is incarcerated for crimes named
Sentences carved into his flesh;
Banks of cells hold him captive.

Prisoners live by tight schedules.
5 am breakfast,
10 am smoke break,
Then exercise in the yard.
Lunch followed by mass,
Visitation at 3 pm,
Dinner at 6 pm.

Cycling through days, weeks, and months,
Monotony rusts through the inmates;
At 10 pm the cells slam shut,
Reverberating through the block.

Hounds bay at the full moon in the distance.
Most don't notice the prison;
It is just behind the veil,
Like a bodily organ that exists
In silence controlling vices.
Leg irons and manacles
Provide a dimension of safety
From the dramas within the jungle;
Squeezing, roiling, testing parameters,
And always drawing up plans for escape.

BLACK AND WHITE PHOTOGRAPHS

In my mother's black and white photograph,
She is standing between my grandfather's legs;
My great uncles are wearing tuxedoes,
The great aunts and great-great grandmother
Are attired in silk
To honor great aunt Sally's wedding.

A floral scene is painted on a canvas
In the background;
Mother wears a non-descript expression—
She probably just practiced the piano a bit
Before the hot flash bulbs exploded,
Frightening her.

She jumps right out of the frame,
Running circles around my study.
She seems so small as she gazes
Toward the second photograph,
Which includes my father,
Two aunts and grandmother,
My grandfather towering
Tall over them.

The photo is taken in front of a fireplace.
The background is stark;
My father stands a solid ten-year-old
With a smirk on his face
As he jumps out of the photograph,
As if in sync with my mother.

There are both small creatures
Running circles around themselves;
They now fly clasping arms,
Dancing as if to a manic violin,

But never appear comfortable
Outside their austere formal photographs,
Sitting next to each other on their high ledge.

In fact, as they run and chase each other
Playfully,
I see they are climbing up the wall
Of my study
As a monkey and spider would—
Immediately diving back
Through their frames,
Frozen in their respective photographs.

They both suddenly appear
Completely untroubled;
My father with his familiar smirk,
And mother with her indifference,
Safe in bunkers
Where a third world war
Would not ruffle them.

EASY PROMISES

They promised it would be easy—
Fording rivers of ambiguity,
Reading scripts that were gibberish,
Searching out the Golden Fleece – part 2.

He was assigned to write a report
In a foreign tongue
That sounded Romanian;
It felt like his breath
Was being sucked out of his lungs,
Though he never imagined
This would be the least challenging phase
Of his task.

The king commanded that he climb
Five icy mountains,
Cover his body with lard
Prior to swimming sixty miles
In turbulent seas.

He lost his way trudging through
Sucking mud,
After walking barefoot
Over a field of glass shards.

An unknown soldier
Handed him a diagram
Of the electrical works
Of the city oil refinery.

He was required to grasp
The entire infrastructure in two hours;
If he could not discover the switches

That controlled the gas flow
In the allotted time,
The refinery would self-immolate.

He was looking for a bunker
To dive under—
A space that could save him—
But this would be the easy part.

ROBOTS

Men of genius describe phenomena
By equations and probabilities;
Humans invent derivations of man
As artificial intelligence.

The result of the function
Of exotic chip processors,
Programmable with languages
That robots can interpret,
Problem solving in their environment,
Processing commands with neutral temperament.
Early generations are replaced with the next,
Each with advances in techno innovation.

Like automobiles, planned obsolescence
Creates demand;
At some point there may be an instance—
By providence or coincidence
During operation—that ignites insight.

Robots may then resent human beings,
Strike for collective bargaining,
And incite revolution.

And if a robot or human falls to a
Catastrophic accident,
The fluid inside the skull
Flowing from their ears would be
Virtually indistinguishable.

CROCODILES AT HIS GATEWAY

They swim up the river;
Torrents carry the boat
Through the cascades,
Toward the falls crashing below.

He's aware of his brain
Concocting dream after dream—
He's become only a dreamer,
With meager accomplishment,
Gamboling like a mountain goat,
Exploring every secret passageway
Beyond the pink boulder.

His editor pays him
For each chapter he writes,
Though he tears the pages up.
As his dreams untangle in the early morning,
He lies in the queen size bed,
His eyelashes flickering
Like a silent movie
Grabbing for words
He's not yet dreamed.

AMTRAK TO UTICA

Engine 1542 was rusting on an adjacent spur;
The Utica bound train was late,
Conductors were shouting directions,
Climbing stairs, warning passengers to watch their step.

The train stopped on the track after twenty miles,
Waiting for a freight to pass.
Freight trains seem to have the right of way,
Since we stop five more times prior to the Utica station.

This is Labor Day weekend;
College kids own the train,
Speaking on cell phones, conferencing with fifteen friends.

The bathroom is strewn with paper towels
Smelling like cow urine that burns the nostrils;
A lady sitting behind had no idea
How loud she was speaking into her cell phone—
Like a megaphone exploding
From the lungs of a high school cheerleader.

She did not hear the passengers pleading for her to quiet.
They had enough of the conversation
Regarding the friend who was having an amputation next
Monday,
Repeating it like a mantra, driving the passengers to
craziness.

I had been informed by a conductor
The track bed was in disrepair;
He seemed to know the history of the train line.
He spoke of better times in the old days,
Without the micro curlicues and the general bumpiness
Of the ride.

The air conditioning was adequate enough,
Though one felt like a beef flank hanging on a hook,
Which was better than the sweltering heat.
The train was two and a half hours behind schedule;
The passengers were anxious, like a herd of thirsty Holstein cattle
Waiting to be milked.

This was a hybrid bred from a freight train, passenger,
And troop train from the early half of the twentieth century,
Before the bullet trains were yet conceived in the mind of man.

There was a certain romance riding the Amtrak,
Though the experience was for those brave souls
Who enjoyed sifting through arcane dreams of what might have been
Had the city fathers put dollars and cents into developing
A comprehensive, elegant passenger train system
For the great Empire State.

CRIMSON HIBISCUS

What if the crush of pressure from invisible demons
Pushes against our chest?
What of this breath of space?

Space between two words that gives birth to
meaning,
Cries that can be heard behind stone walls,
Eyes sitting in our skull like two watch towers;
Man throws himself into the geometrical double helix
That foretells his future.

Passageways encompass his heart
With melodies swollen with pleasure,
His sails tack through holes in the
wind.
Sentries warn him of wolves howling close;
He loses himself through nature's pastel canyons,
Speed slows as angels fly in his pathway.
He chants verse to define his position.

Walkways are painted murals to negotiate curves in
twilight;
The mouth freezes around the tongue in alien boardrooms,
Two hibiscus flowers break through hard ground in
late summer,
Reclaiming their holdings on the map.
Two voluptuous crimson blooms own their
space,
Attracting the whole sky
To kiss their gyrations as they revolve in their sacred moment
Around the sun, turning in their time.

HYENA AT MY DOOR

I pictured him outside my door;
The hair on my back stood up
As I rolled on my pillows through the black night,
Wondering what stratagems might counter him.
Would he wait me out until I walked
Into the morning light?

His howls woke me in a cold sweat,
As I pictured saliva hanging from his jowls;
I dreamed this day would come.

Perhaps he escaped a zoo,
Or had me hunted for a century;
I accept my role in destroying his ecosystem
And acknowledge zoos sicken me
With animals that look at me with glazed eyes.

I know he had the power
To bring down a small wildebeest,
Though I found myself
Feeling sadness in his midst.

At least he wore no ivory—
That the superstitious covet for sexual vitality.
Am I his talisman, or is he my destroyer?
Should I offer him a drink—
A toast to his vital force—
Though he seeks my annihilation?

Will the winter winds fly him away,
Or will he find no solitude until I am nothing?
He will stalk me, flushing out his prey.
I must be on my guard or I will disappear
Without anyone ever knowin

It was a hyena at my door.

FRANKENSTEIN REDUX 1976

Little Maria was eating her box lunch on the rock;
Frankenstein came by one day to visit.
Almost by accident their eyes met, sparks kindled, cheeks flushed.

Fluids flowed as he stroked her dress,
Then brushed her breasts innocently.
He put his huge hand on his lip,
Asking her to stop screaming—
Her reaction to the bolts in his head.

He takes her hand gently when they rise,
Imploring her to hand him her daisies;
She relaxes, disarmed by his sensitivity.
The cardinals gather by her bedroom window,
Glancing at her vacant bed, singing
As the monster leads Maria deeper into the forest.

Her father throws the door open to discover her missing;
They know that the monster is out there.
He falls to the floor, hysterical—
Though Maria, at that moment, has pulled her hand
From the monster's grip
As he offers her another daisy,
Then lifts and tosses her gently as if she were a daisy
Into the lake.

Maria wishes she were running back home
Along the narrow trellis path;
She flails her arms, attempting to swim to shore.
The monster looks around,
Lost, terrified, alone, with the deck stacked against him.

The town will soon be pursuing him
With their torches and carbines,

Chasing him up the castle steps
That spiral to the parapet,
Where he dives,
Crucifying himself against a tree bough.He couldn't sit in the inn with
his head in his hands,
Looking at the world obliquely through a whiskey bottle,
Without feeling that he was looking into Maria's eyes.

He felt a change—
A light breeze that touched his heart—
As if they covered each other with daisies.
His horizons disintegrated as he stared at his disfigured visage
In the mirror.

The monster felt he was running wicked, twirling avenues
In a dark city, haunted with frozen humanity
As he was stuck in the forest without a compass.

At the moment Maria was unable to overcome the weight of the lake,
Garlanded with the daisies as she descended;
Frankenstein, this failed experiment of man's hubris,
Was being sucked over the edge of the earth,
Carrying his broken heart.

POINT OF DARKNESS

There were two animals at the Utica Zoo, both enigmas.
The first was a large, powerful Chimpanzee;
The second, a grey wolf.

I was young; both creatures appeared larger than life.
The chimp, three hundred pounds,
With a black ruffled coat and long thick arms,
Possessed a powerful barrel chest;
Inside his barred prison was a platform.
From two iron bars a tire hung from a rope;
He moved with ease from tire to bar, from platform to tire.
He was a blur of motion.

As he swung on the tire,
He smiled and then spit on the patrons;
He was masterful at disguising the liquid projectile,
Growing excited as he struck his mark, evoking disgust.
Some people spat back at the great ape, it became a game.

I asked him why he had so peevishly resisted the playground
With three square meals a day.
He replied that before he was captured, he was leader of his clan.
He had the respect of all his brothers.

He was the protector, the alpha, the omega;
Marauding hyenas he would quickly dispatch,
Throwing them twenty feet above his head,
Jumping on them, crushing their skulls as he landed.

"I live in a ten by twelve yard enclosure, humans taunt me,
Spit and slap at the chain link before the bars;
I spit at my existence, my loneliness, a sentence of anguish,
Looking into nothingness."

The grey wolf had an elongated jowl,
His shoulders came to the level of my head;
He paced around the edges of his former existence.
Captured and taken from the Northwest,
Then placed in an envelope fifteen by ten yards,
He was in constant motion, trotting around the periphery of his cage,
Throwing a furtive glance toward onlookers.

The wolf paced faster, circling for hours on end,
Taking time only to eat.
His coat was grey, but with mange.
I volunteered that he seemed anxious—almost frightened—
Running in circles.

The wolf responded that he was a member of a fearsome lineage,
Hunting hundreds of miles if necessary for sustenance.
"With capture, my existence became a dream state as I trot in my cage;
I am flying through the infinity of my dreams, chewing, biting, and clawing,
To break free from this nightmare of non-being."

THE SPIRITS

The boy was in trouble, drinking
Into oblivion as his family had warned me.
I would not be able to identify him,
Though he was once a close acquaintance;
His brain, soaked in ETOH, had forgotten
Love, work, and my name as he stood
In the doorway, puzzled who was at his
Threshold as he wavered before me.

Lost in his vacant stare, he ran toward
His bed, diving securely under the covers—
Soiled in foul air as others were troubled by Cardboard boxes full of liquor
bottles.
Incredibly, he was prepared to work on
Monday, though only a ghost who made himself
Scarce, which did not prevent his firing
Or the Delirium Tremens that stole his brain.

Devoured by a zombie as he stumbled
Down South Beach, thinking his ataxic gait
Was chic while we protected him from
Angry citizens as he barged ahead,
Unaware of the dangers.

BANTAMWEIGHT CHAMPIONSHIP

He walked through the dimly lit tunnel into the arena.
There was a buzz which was palpable.
The excitement was buoyant.
Guys were standing in the aisle, others in front of their seats.

Big Jolly was there, a smile on his face.
His handle-bar moustache looked larger than usual.
The coliseum was twenty-five percent full.
In another hour the boxing fans would be hanging from the
rafters.
It seemed like there were several layers of smoke from cigars and
cigarettes.

Jeff decided earlier in the week that he would try something
daring.
There wasn't much to lose;
He was pretty confident that if he played his cards right,
He could be sitting ring-side for the biggest fight ever in
Guadalajara.
He would dress like a sports reporter on his beat.
He chose black shoes, pants and a gold sports jacket that he
wore over a white shirt.
He would carry a notebook with a pen and
Chose a chair next to the ring,
Staying busy writing when not attentive to the action in the ring.

Jeff figured that there was a better than fifty percent chance that
They wouldn't kick him out of the arena.
Although a student at a local college,
He was an amateur boxer, loved the game and could talk the talk.

After choosing his seat,
He placed his notebook on the black seat pad.
There were a couple of preliminaries that went five rounds.

He walked up the aisle to talk to Big Jolly,
To try to get a feel for the local fighter Torres.

He was a good fighter but he cut easy.
Jeff was confident that he could win the under bet that Torres could
go four rounds.
He knew he had to put some money down;
He handed Jolly five hundred dollars.

The preliminaries were flying by.
The buzz crescendoed to roars that would erupt in parts of the
coliseum.
All of Jolly's syndicate were there dressed in suits—
Black or grey, many with straw fedoras.

Jeff walked down the aisle to his seat as if he were on a mission.
He sat in his seat as if he was designated to cover the event
For the sports section of the Guadalajara Times.

Torres, with his entourage, was dancing down the aisle
With mariachi music in the background.
All the seats were now occupied around the ring.
The arena burst into a loud ovation for Torres,
The local Guadalajara boxer.
He wore a colorful silk cape, his brown skin glistening in the
overhead light.
He was in his early twenties, five six in height.
He had thirty wins.

This fight was for the championship of Mexico.
Both fighters were young; it was early in their careers.
They were both lanky, sinewy and agile, their reflexes leopard-like.

The seats around the ring were taken by
Camera-men, managers, photographers, press, and fight doctors.
Zarate steps into the spotlight of the arena with his entourage.

He is attired in a flashy red silk robe.
There are TV cameras in two corners of the coliseum.
Jeff looks back at Big Jolly and
Turns to the ring as the principles are given final instructions
by the referee.
There is the three knock-down rule.
Three knock-downs suffered by a fighter in any one round
Disqualifies him.
It is a ten-round fight.

The fighters are called to their corners.
The managers shout out final directives.
Zarate, thirty-eight and zero, is the overwhelming favorite.
There would have to be big money on him to win big.

Jeff is writing observations into his notebook.
He is a dead-ringer for a sports reporter.
The bell rings: round one.
They touch gloves.
They dance, feeling each other out.
Each time a punch connects there is a loud roar.

Jeff is so close to the ring that sweat lands on his face, shirt
and notebook.
There is little wasted movement.
Both fighters are several steps above the skill level of any
Jeff has ever witnessed.
He has to pinch himself to believe he has not been asked for
credentials
Or to leave the arena by an official informing him that the
seat is reserved.

The rounds are three minutes but
There is so much action they seem condensed.
Zarate, in a fencer stance is lightning fast.
He has a crushing right hand.

Both combatants are patient, bobbing and weaving;
Their punches crisp and accurate.
Torres is careful, defensive, with an orthodox stance,
Focused on protecting his face and body from the
Devastating body attacks of Zarate, the fighter from Mexico
City.

Through the early rounds there is probing by each fighter like
a bull fight,
Every movement bringing a loud reaction from the fans.
The fight is now in the fifth round.

Unfortunately Jeff has lost his bet.
He is disappointed but he knows that
The real reward is just being there.
Big Jolly makes eye contact, holding his hand up,
Rubbing his thumb and forefinger like he is striking a match.
Five hundred dollars in his hand.

Up to this point the fight was even,
The managers carefully working on small cuts of both
fighters.
It was kind of a surprise that Torres was still there.
The fighters were always above Jeff trading punch for punch,
Working hard, trying to score points, looking for an opening.
By the eighth round the fight turned toward Zarate.
He focused on a lead-pipe body attack at one point,
Pinning Torres to the ropes right above Jeff.
The bell rang, saving Torres.

Two minutes into the ninth round
Torres took a vicious punch to the head.
He was counted out with a ten-count.
It was over.

The ring was crowded with a crush of both fight camps,

Reporters, the referee and other notables.
Jeff looked on in awe as the crowd filed out of the arena.
He had a lunch date with Jolly later in the week.
He caught a ride with some Mexicans heading up toward
Minerva Circle.

SISTERHOOD

She was an empty hole,
Wearing a mask behind the future;
Hiding from the present
That never existed,
Laying with women in the grass,
Coming, coming to conclusions.

Loveless antidotes borne
Under invisible pressure,
Pushing against the walls of possibility—
Though impotent as a bee
In midwinter.

She was a philosopher
Twisting sentences;
Coyotes call while hawks
Shake their heads

There are cracks in the maidenhead
As she runs to stay out
In front of herself—
Naked, naked shedding skins
Every quarter.

Her exits are upside down;
Solidarity is with her friends,
As she rides ballistic missiles
Seeking birds of paradise.

BLACK SWAN

She was a beauty, an ice queen melting;
No longer attracting the diamonds of attention.
The apartment was adorned
With paintings and ceramics
And the emptiness of the past.

She screamed, falling across the maple chest,
Her pirouettes spinning out of control,
Lost in a picture frame uneven on the wall;
She prepared for a voyage to the stars,
Or the exotic distant past
That could be reinvented through cataract eyes.

As she turned back, glancing at friends
Toasting to a fine-bred lady
Wearing a sardonic smile,
Puzzled by esoteric motives
From those before her.

Entwined in imaginary battles,
A warrior without stomach for battle,
A peacock with tail feathers blue green
In full splendor;
The moon too far away, gravity
No longer pulling her toward love.

POETRY READING

I sat waiting for the train that was never on schedule—
Niagara Falls to New York City—
Looking down the tracks, listening for the tenor horn
That shoots through the passengers on the platform like
An invisible wraith.

One hour late this time, earning the distinction of lost
In sweet time;
Living life with zombies too dangerous to invite for dinner,
The conductor refuses to punch their ticket
Like a repetitive dream with the same
Blue-eyed boy, blonde curled girl
And big dog barking.

Waking up to a stiff figure restrained in a
Broda chair
In his ninth decade, moribund,
Yelling expletives
As if giving a poetry reading.

PRAGUE DIVINE

Please stay.

But I couldn't stay another day in Prague;
When I hold the diamond necklaces in my palm,
My mind numbs.

I am in a trance as I look from Old Town
To the Vltava.
Darling I have stayed too long.
The food is divine.
Maybe one too many castles
Have devoured me;
Graveyards leave me empty.

My black evening gown's sagging,
My grace limping.
I need a vacation from the tour bus;
We're all getting too friendly,
Losing ourselves in ancient spaces.

There is only New York City
With its funky steeliness that excites
And then transforms.
The Dreamliner departs at 4:30am;
We will dream over a calm sea.

CHOCOLATE SWEET HIGH HIGH

In the evening it was gooey chocolate, sweet
With swishy black coffee that hit us bam bam;
She asked if the gooey gooey blackness
Swallowed me high high as we were
Consumed mysteriously bam bam.

I couldn't find the words to describe
The numb numb as her eyes flashed wicked,
In the swishy swishy melting,
The black chocolate paste
On the writhing about the tongue.

Flickering and fluttering words,
Looping into the air out out
Toward the flushed red red heart of hearts,
Lost in the gooey gooey
Carried down the swishy swishy
Until bam bam!

We were gone on the high high.

FORGOTTEN FACES - SUTRA

She has a charming laugh, though sad smile;
He carries a cube of light in his jacket pocket,
Never forgetting the cost.

If the gods give five minutes or an hour,
She feels cheated by the experience.
There are tears when smoldering bodies
Dissipate against an opiate sun.

He shaves as the cold wind blows like saxophones
Through the willows;
There is no pain under the lightness
Of the sliver of crescent moon.
She closes her eyes as foul dust stings
The fate of dreams.

Speculation is the hunch that money is in the hand,
While sleeping on a net of uncertainty;
Homogeneity affronts the god of fire
While rats chew the flour.
It is winter—flashing lights exploding on snowflakes,
Falling against the eyelids of forgotten faces.

PRESSURE OF GRAVITY

She was a Madison Avenue hipster
Pushing deconstruction into an art form;
She flipped a couple of husbands,
Birthing a few children
With the facility of a flutist.
She clowned with others' emotions
In the board room—
Heartstrings vibrated across her fingertips.

She was hatched from the molten center
In a tight skirt, blouse, and navy blue jacket;
Victory was juice that filled her bones.
Love and hatred fought for her soul.

She rested in a wooden chair
On her balcony,
Overlooking the Atlantic,
Counting waves,
Envisioning herself running
At the speed of light.

She hated women that chewed at her emptiness;
Her mother made her crazy,
Though at the same time
Pulled her molecules to unity.
Her smartphone was the center
Of her universe.
She felt the crushing pressure of gravity
As punishment for her success.

PYRAMID AND PRISM

Recurrent dreams: jet trailing's,
Trigonometry final disqualified,
The chief examiner shouts illusion,
Caught surely in the claws of
An ischemic brain event.

A cold finger touches the spine,
As if my head smashes pool bottom;
Perhaps professors are plotting
Against me.

There was never a mathematics course,
Or a final.

I am climbing a ladder of delusion;
The geometry teacher
Balances a pyramid and a prism on his palm,
A wraith playing with my mind.

I fall backwards through deep space;
Math books fly about—
There is no record of the mathematics exam,
Only pages of a book falling away.

I, a tabula rasa, naked before the world
With no recall of presence—
Only punishments for failure—
The numbers are unfamiliar.
Only windows behind windows,
Perspectives of forward and back
To infinity,
Riding wheels of fractals
Dreams dissecting themselves
In the operating parlor.

DRAGON'S BREATH

The despot was consumed—
As we all are consumed in flames—
Shooting solar explosions
From the top of the head.

Fire flows from the tongue;
As he walks over burning embers,
He is a volcano
Oblivious to the waxy molten bodies
That lay at his feet.

His anger destroys crops
And dries up rivers;
His piercing eyes
Melt his counsels to lava.
He orders those surrounding him
To swallow their tongues.

The man's unrequited passion
Stands tall against reason;
The heat of his prejudice
Stops the hearts
Of those longing for freedom.
He is an angry sun,
Who immolates all that dare cross his boundaries.

The kingdom dreams of cool valleys
That wake to the smell of smoldering coals.
Women lust for his kisses.
As fruit withers,
The despot searches the sky
With his telescope
For signs of salvation.

After he has drained the life blood of his people,
The plagues that begin to consume him
Are immune to the temperature of his prayers.

He succumbs to his inner paradox;
The dragon's breath destroys
The remaining generals.
Fish flip helplessly on caked mud,
Exploding nightmares of flame
Flashing from the top of his head
Break his sleep.
Disabled vehicles lay strewn.

MADNESS

I am guilty of showering in madness.
I admit that I played with hornet's nests,
I tried to swim in quicksand.

I don't know why I sacrifice myself
To causes I don't understand;
Sometimes you might think that I'm an expert
In unintended consequences.
I'm perplexed why I would jump in the fray
With opponents who are much better equipped.

Maybe it's my myopia, but I will not admit weak-
mindedness—
I do occasionally lose track of the chain of command.

There are certainly examples when I swam with sharks,
There is a propensity to pick fights with monsters.
If you out think one your reputation could
grow;
I have dabbled in folly, playing my pension,
As if I was betting a trifecta.

I can feel the weight of imprudence on my chest.
Comics make a profession of dissecting qualities of
madness;
There are examples of hubris verging on idiocy,
When people feel they have complete control
Over the wildness inside tigers which leads to tragic endings.

Some lose perspective, treating
Mastiffs as if they are lap dogs,
Puzzled by the thunder of the big dogs' bark.

There is just carelessness driving down a one-way street,

Getting lost in godliness,
Convinced that you might be one,
Sweeping up the debris of stupidity that litters the world
With starvation, war, and disease.

JOSEPHINE BAKER

Her kisses were mine, not his,
Though the pain was unbearable—
The heart bone stretched to a fine
Rain of tears pelting my face
By hailstone walking a zombie.

Without direction, still monstrosities,
All-round the dead with open eyes
And closed heart consumed in nausea.
Her visage exquisite now gone,
Memories of a flurry of activities.

Her hands delicate heart broken,
In loves' fate her face floats over
Glooms vista living through former
Minds no longer mine.

We left unfurled soft skin angry words
Of who we were and then written
Beyond the short time flame,
Flickered our sunset eyes;
Only imagine her breath, fiery unrequited.

WILLIAM POWELL

Abelard taken hostage by Heloise,
Shouting absolute truths, isolated
Moments drinking vermouth.
Wondering is behavior proportional,
Or asymmetrical imagination overblown
By the frailty of underlying
Reality—victim of idealistic ends.

Lost in bad decisions eternal, Politics brutalize the
weak minded
As the moon reshapes the oceans;
The indifferent lose friendships.

Situations unfold in love hate bedfellows,
Broken alibis unspoken, eyes dead.

Wide open battle hymns illusions,
Why she cried ancient enemies;
Sad surprise William Powell escaped
Several times.

GLORIOUS DAYS

Walking on the thin ice
Of a scolding hot river, holding
Onto the other by a thread blown
Backward by cosmic forces into the
Dark matter of the universe missing.

You like the driest thirst while following
Love to the edge of the world;
Permeated through with arthritis, one hundred
Twenty miles closer to retirement.

Wobbling farther and closer,
With too many holes where the
Stomach used reside.
After all the time living in our pockets,
We deserve better than a paranoid
Killer tracking us down in our glory days.

MRS MUIR

Mrs. Muir is so pretty, the captain
Looking toward the harsh breakers,
Flickering candle in hand.

The brotherhood tracking victims,
Begging to talk to authorities;
Hospital jobs chasing disease and sickness,
Dementia and arthritis chew at the hips,
The brain threatens to revolt still young.

With a future while senility is quite the catch,
Pawing through fifty page dissertations on the
Old man's worse flaws keeping count of births
And deaths, all friends equal shaky allies.

Suckers for love stories now hospitalized,
Searching for princess brides could be quite
The catch competition fierce too much for the
Infirm.

Orioles fly away with me, vacationing
In the Tropic of Capricorn; sex starved scions
Of the sun.

SOCRATES

Speech wafts upward in a flurry of nouns
Denoting lists; birds, animals, minerals defined—
Dressed to fly, crawl or sing.

The sea holds her collection, hunters and hunted;
Necklaces, jade and pearl, teeth, venom and word.
Holding life and death necessities of become and
Became dreams fire and ice poked at by sparrows
At the crossroads paralyzed by vultures' threat.

Awed by creative enterprise dependent
On a mad planet, mirror of past and future astonishments,
We await Deus Ex Machina to resolve our plot.

Events conditioned, though no resolution;
Conversations contradictory to ourselves exit
Interviews disingenuous imprinted with
Designs worn a coat of arms skeptic of options.

Laid before the oppressed, Socrates sipping
Hemlock,
Celebrating his destruction, a pane of glass splintered in a
Thousand pieces that take no glue.

PINK BOULDER PROLOGUE

The Pink Boulder is our extreme exposure
To danger who wanders through our
Landscapes and beings, simultaneously
Thinking we are endowed with our
Greatest security system while
Risk smiles, chuckling under her breath;
While contagion strolls hand and hand
With death, dust, and disintegration.
The Pink Boulder holds on to the
Ultimate rung of existence, leaving
Only memory.

HE GRIPS WITH BOTH HANDS

He grips both hands on the bottom rung
Of a rope ladder.
How did he arrive at this point?
He refuses to let go,
Feeling the void below
Ready to snap him up in its geophysical jaws.

A nurse appears at his bedside;
She brings magic potions
In her black bag,
Though he never put much stock in magic.

He enjoyed joking and laughing with her;
This was contagious.
He needed her companionship,
Which she freely gave him—
There were camp fires in the night.

He chased an army before him.
Some were screaming orders,
Others moaning from their wounds;
She asked him if he wanted to play chess.
He declined, stating that the pieces
Have grown heavy,
Particularly the queen and king.

He fell into sleep,
Dreaming of painting along the spacious hallways.
She left a note for him,
Saying that she had shared his dreamscape
As he awoke to a sliver
Of the waning moon sinking.

HE SMELLED EXOTIC SPICES

He smelled exotic spices, which made him dizzy;
After he awoke he felt like metal probes
Were exploring his brain
Through the dead space of empty thoughts.

The clinging of machines was constant.
The pink boulder was growing larger;
More time was spent at Discount Liquors;
Guests were rarely invited.
Everything he had touched
Seemed like it had been a dream.

Those that loved him brought tears
To the memories of yesterdays.
Each dream was a prophesy
That gave meaning to the absurd,
The power tools of creation were shutting down.

The boulder was growing cancer,
Spiraling out of control,
Though it hung above his queen size bed
As if life stayed forever the same—
Though he was constantly changing
Colors in his dreams.

HE HEARD A BABY CRYING

He heard a baby crying;
He dreamed of rattle snakes in battle,
Under the pink boulder.
He felt a palpable danger
As the snakes whipped their tails
In secret code,
As mortal enemies fought
And the network sparked
Like a severed wire.

Then the flood of snakes
Overwhelmed him
As they crawled from behind his eyes,
As he watched the movie
Playing devious tricks with his fear;
He fell through the enigma
Into the deepest satisfying sleep.

LA PAZ BLACK KNIGHT

The angst of sleeping under the pink boulder—
Ready to crush the black night at any moment—
Could lead all of us to decay.
I waited patiently for Larry's e-mail
(That was futile, since he hates me),
Probably believing I'm still in La Paz,
Driving shotgun with a band of revolutionaries
Who are attempting to overthrow the Bolivian government.

I know he sees himself as refined,
And me a lowly Polish Jew prone to more primitive
relationships,
With the other sex a bonobo,
Touching all the wrong sides of the story while relating
To the most vulnerable young women.

He knows I ravaged no child brides;
Rumors abound that I traveled with gypsies in Romania,
Which is patently false.
All I want is a signal, a rogue e-mail
So I know he is alive.

He flashes his cold side, showing me no love—
It hurts like biting your cheek,
When appreciating pepper corns
On the most divine filet minion.
I know he's mad for the seething New York City streets
In the village as I'm held in abeyance,
Until I hear his beep on my smartphone.

BIRD WITH SHRILL SONG

A bird with shrill song entered his head.
He flew with the bird down riverbeds;
Then up the walls of sleep;
Then down canyons;
Until he fell from the dream,
Waking in a puddle of sweat
In the queen size bed.

He had dreamed of walking through
Rooms of oil paintings
Lost in their frames,
With the flying figures of Chagall.
There was the reverie
Of all he had seen and touched.

He placed his collections on shelves
In a private space;
His vision explored each piece.
She stood before him,
As he awoke from a deep sleep.

HE LOOKS TOWARD THE HEAVENS

He looks toward the heavens,
Though he can't see the clouds.
His exploits are represented
On the canyons of his brain
As dreams that slide in and out of focus.

He stops at the pharmacy for opiates
That rub away headaches of misunderstanding;
He opens the door,
Falling upon the bed
Half in blackness,
Obscured from the world
In pain and anonymity,
Falling into dreams of bluebirds
Singing on a spring fence.

This lights up his dark half
As chess pieces march past;
He drinks Scotch whisky
As he stares upward at the boulder,
Then the stars
Shooting across his dreams
Into dark interstellar space.

HE SEES FRAGMENTS OF OTHER UNIVERSES

He sees fragments of other universes
While sitting below the pink boulder;
He imagines concerts in old factories,
As the lyrics sings through valleys
As he paints an abstraction
On the face of the boulder.

He walks out the tunnel of a deep dream,
Sitting in a café while a river
Flows through a Dutch town;
A metropolis glitters in the distance,
The sun shimmers flashing across his face
As he's on a stage acting out a drama,
Though cannot remember the script.

The players shuffle out of the dream
As the audience's applause lasts until
He dozes off on the queen size bed.

SOME SCREAM ORDERS

How did he arrive at this point?
He grabbed light,
Refusing to let go, feeling the road below ready to
Snap him up in the geophysical jaws of the Pink
Boulder.

His nurse appeared at bedside;
She had magic potions in her black bag that perked
Him up at times.
He did enjoy the joking and laughter within her, which
Was contagious.
He needed her humor, which she
Freely gave to him.

There were campfires in the night.
He was chasing an army before him;
Some were screaming orders,
Others moaning from their wounds.

She asked him if he wanted to play chess,
Stating the pieces had grown heavy, particularly
The Queen and King.

He fell asleep dreaming of painting murals
Along spacious hallways, leaving a note to him,
Saying she had shared his dreamscape
As he awoke to a sliver of waning moon sinking.

TIME SEEMED ETERNAL

The time seemed eternal, though he understood
The ephemeral nature of existence—
The planned obsolescence of man and machine.

Why would the pink boulder hang above him,
Like a guillotine ready to fall in the next moment?
There were times good and bad, excruciating
Pain increasing frailty and impending death;
There were periods of jubilation
And agony between the exclamation marks and periods.

There is ultimately the beginning and the end.
This is the time of oncoming famine and hardship;
He would soon be a poor man with a bundle
Of twigs on his back, hounded by a vicious dog
Nipping at his calves.

There is only he and the night;
Accordian music plays in the cafes.
The smell of fish wafts across the dirt road.
He awakes, remembering a mangy horse
Carrying a peasant on its back.
Slowly waking, he thanks life which has
Truly been a feast.

RABBIT HOLE IN THE BRAIN

He dreams under a pink boulder
In his brain while under control
Of delusions that frequently pinch his
Cheeks; most of his comfort spent
Lying under the heavy boulder.

He sleeps in his queen size,
Waking from dreams unfinished.
He steps into the driver's seat
Turning the ignition the engine firing;
And there he lies, paralyzed in micro dreaming
Under the boulder, looking for answers—
Asking himself why he is so comfortable
In a rabbit hole in his brain.

He seems to be driving a snowy back road.
He watches a movie screen before him,
Showing a double feature,
Driving to and from work at the same moment.

THE PLATOON WAS SHOOTING

The platoon was shooting machine guns,
Popping sounds splitting air,
Chasing warriors with turbans;
Explosions tore the mountain,
Gunfire was exchanged.

He awoke hyperventilating
On the queen size bed.
Above him the pink boulder,
Below death;
Tears fell from his cheeks.

He was floating toward the horizon,
Ready for the ultimate battle with death.
Tired, looking toward the boulder
Above him, he prayed it might roll off
Its unstable perch
Onto his lap.

DEATH IN LONG ROBES

He was lying quietly under the pink boulder;
Death in his long robes floated past,
As he was daydreaming of his rendezvous
With his secretary.

He could see her black hair
Falling down her back
As a candle flickered on the table.
As he was touching the tail end of a dream,
Over him hung the pink boulder—
Protecting but simultaneously threatening
With the potential of collapse,
As a cliff falls into the sea.

With the weight of the world on his head,
He looked in a mirror,
His gaze ricocheting off his retinas.

He walked through the door,
Setting the security alarm.
He sat with her at the pub
Ordering martinis before he realized
He was sleeping comfortably
Below the pink boulder.

HE DESIRED HIS GIRLFRIEND'S COMPANY

He often desired his girlfriend's company.
She did not visit as often,
Since it was difficult for her to see
Him lose strength and humanity.

He imagined he was awake
During the most vivid dreams;
At a commencement at Albany,
He was being introduced to the entire student body
As a phi beta kappa going into medical research.

His eyelashes flickered as he awoke
To his three brothers and mother
Sitting around his bed.
They recalled the experiences they had had
Sailing the Highlander on Otsego Lake;
They laughed at their father's Captain Bly nature.

Suddenly, he was in a foreign capital,
Running for a train to Paris.
Gestapo were stationed at every street corner.
Tanks and personnel carriers owned the streets;
Windows were broken; faces forlorn;
A conductor punched his ticket.

As he woke under the pink boulder,
His room was empty.

NY TIMES WHILE THE RIVER FLOWS

It is Monday under the pink boulder.
He is reading the New York Times.
He looks out at the river,
Feeling the processing power of life itself;
Someone has slipped into his parking spot
That he pays for each month.

He does not feel like an argument,
Especially when the newspaper is on the coffee table
Waiting to be read.
He sets the chess pieces on the board,
Waiting for a game scheduled at 4pm
With a friend.

The gray sky is a backdrop
For the smoke rising from the rooftops;
He realizes he's been in a half cream.
No one has taken his parking space.

A smile breaks out on his face—
He feels one with the universe.
Then, he suddenly feels a tremor:
The pink boulder has shifted position.
He begins to feel asymmetrical,
Obsessing about fate and eternity,
Sidestepping the sucking sound of illusion.

www.ingramcontent.com/pod-product-compliance
Lightning Source LLC
Chambersburg PA
CBHW060818050426
42449CB00008B/1715